story by Cheryl Ryan
illustrations by Ethan Long

HARCOURT BRACE & COMPANY

Orlando   Atlanta   Austin   Boston   San Francisco   Chicago   Dallas   New York
Toronto   London

Thursday is show and tell day.

I know what I'm going to bring.
It's a big secret.

Only my friend Josh knows what it is.

"We'll keep it a secret," I said.

Then I had to tell my teacher.

"Want to know a secret?" I asked.

But Julie and Matthew wondered and wanted to know.

"You must keep it a secret," I said.

I think a few others heard us.

But I wanted it to be a secret!

I was ready on Thursday.

"Here's my secret show and tell!"

My mom walked into the room.

Everyone looked and wondered.

My secret started to cry.
I think she even surprised herself!
"It's my new sister!"

Teacher/Family Member: ································

Have children explain what a secret is and name some good
ways to keep a secret private.

•••

Word count:	114
Vocabulary:	*wondered, herself*
Phonic Elements:	*R*-controlled vowel: /ûr/*er, ur ;* Short vowel: /u/*u*

ISBN 0-15-307884-7

Ordering Options
ISBN 0-15-308197-X (Package of 5)
ISBN 0-15-306426-9 (Grade 2 Package)

678910 139 99 98